UNDERSTANDING HOW TO EXECUTE THE STRATEGY

A Ten Step Protocol for Business Success

(A Business Strategy Publication)

Published by:
Chronicle Publishing
Milwaukee, WI
Cover design by: Demonica Flagg

Printed In the United States of America
ISBN: 978-0-9883298-4-3

Books also by Dr. Valerie Daniels-Carter

- ❖ His Business Is Your Business, It's Where Destiny Takes You.

- ❖ Anointed Offering or Tainted Sacrifice

- ❖ The Journey of a Winner

- ❖ From Pandemic to Promise

The Forward

When I reflect on the many things that I have accomplished over time, I can easily delineate what I believe to be Critical Keys to my Business Success. The first and most important key to my success is God! He is the reason why I exist. He has given me the ability and capacity to do the things that I do. He has gifted and anointed me with skills and proficiencies that allow me to manage and operate in business from day to day. God has seeded wisdom and knowledge within the tentacles of my being, and for this I am Thankful and Grateful!

Secondly, I would not enjoy Success in Business, if it were not for my family and close friends. To have a loving, strong and supportive familial base, individuals who understand the value and importance of destiny...Those who challenge you to execute at the highest degree possible... This is Invaluable I appreciate family, those present, as well as those who have been promoted from this earth. They along with my close friends have served as a foundational rock to me. For this, I am also Grateful!

Next, I must acknowledge my V&J Family. The anchor of my success is hinged on having a team that consistently executes daily. Our motto at V&J is "YATSE" *(You Are the Standard of Excellence)*. I have been blessed and afforded the opportunity to work with employees, who over the years, proven themselves faithful and committed to our stated goals and objectives. Because of their superiority in delivering great results, V&J has been recognized as an industry leader. Thank you for being the support team that makes the vision possible.

Lastly, let me acknowledge my customers, both internal and external. Your continuous support of me and my organization is sincerely and highly appreciated. I could not have made it without you. I am Grateful for every one of you!

NOW, as I end this forward, I want to DEDICATE this book to a very special person. I dedicate it to my business partner and only living sibling, my brother, Attorney John Daniels, Jr.

John is a result-oriented leader and a brilliant world-class attorney. He is skillful and insightful and is recognized as one of the "Who's Who" among attorneys. He is a legal mogul who has executed major business transactions nationwide. Attorney Daniels is an astute businessman. He is not flashy or flamboyant but has a "heart of gold". John is a man who loves his family and humanity; one who seeks to build community and leaders; one who is always seeking ways to improve the lives of others; he is a champion for many, including often serving as a champion for the "underserved." It would take the remainder of this book for me to chronicle his life, corporate, and business achievements, because they are so gigantic. That is John and for those who know John, we appreciate his sincere drive for excellence. I am honored to be his business partner and for over 40 years, we have blazed this business trail together. Let me share a secret with you. The reason why I gleam so, is because John is like an oil press machine that "pushes and presses" you, until your true intrinsic value is released. John, thank you for the "pushing and pressing"! Thank you for being my Hero!

John, you are a true hero in a blighted world that can be challenging. Your unwavering selflessness, and dedication inspire us all. Thank you for your service and sacrifice. Thank you for LOVING ME, BELIEVING IN ME and being not only my big brother, collaborator and confidant; but for being a man of extraordinary courage who motivates countless individuals *to excel and soar above the norm.*

UNDERSTANDING

HOW TO EXECUTE THE

STRATEGY

> ➤ *Nugget* - An "idea" is not a business plan; it is a creative thought.

As with most of my writings, throughout this book, I will share Nuggets of Wisdom (called Nuggets). Nuggets of Wisdom are thoughts that you should ponder and intensely think about.

Primer

"Potential Is Not A Strategy". Potential is having or showing the capacity to become or improve. It is the "current" unrealized ability to accomplish a task or thing. When something is not actualized, it is still considered in the state of possibility and has the ability to become. You must have more than the potential to "Excel Above the Norm". To operate in a place of exceptional performance, yes, you might have the ability; but you must also have a profound understanding of what, when, and how if you are going to move forward productively.

This book is designed to challenge every leader and entrepreneur who desires to operate beyond passion and potential to understand the value and importance of proactively analyzing, creating and outlining an effective written strategy prior to creating or expanding their business.

According to 2024 data from the U.S. Bureau of Labor Statistics [1], "20.4% of businesses fail in their first year after opening, 49.4% fail in their first five years, and 65.3% fail in their first 10 years."

As a leading entrepreneur in America, I have been asked over and over, "How do we change this trajectory?" "How do we ensure a higher level of business success?" Is it possible to reduce the number of small businesses that fail? How does one succeed in this current environment? "

Insights related to these, and other questions will be discussed in subsequent chapters as I unveil the *"Valerie Daniels- Carter (VDC) Ten Step Protocol for Business Success. "*

I created the *"VDC Ten-Step Protocol for Business Success"* as a necessary tool for emerging and expanding enterprise leaders. It encircles a thought-provoking process that allows leaders and entrepreneurs who desire to improve the probability of business success for themselves to engage in. My challenge for those who seek advice from me is to ensure that you can understand and definitively answer every VDC Protocol Category aptly. If you can, then you are clearly headed in a positive and healthy direction.

The goal is for you to strategically and proactively address critical strategic business platforms because it will improve your insight and increase your probability of success. Make sound decisions. No business is 100% fail proof, but you certainly can increase the odds of success if you take time to diligently work through the *VDC Ten Step Protocol for Business Success.*

Here is your first nugget.

> ➤ *Nugget* - *As a great leader, you cannot be afraid to navigate through uncharted territory. But you must be intentional in your approach and have a good sense of direction.*

Having a unique or cutting-edge idea or concept can yield significant opportunity and advancement.

Innovativeness is a jewel that is rarely found, so always remember; the copiousness of your success will be predicated on how well you proactively prepare and position yourself in advance of the undertaking.

It is often asked, "Where does Good Success" come from? Well, I have a very indubitable answer, – It only comes from the God. Now let's extend this narrative....... What happens when you combine God's formula for Good Success with *"The Valerie Daniels-Carter (VDC) Ten Step Business Protocol Platform for Executing Business in Excellence"*?

You Got It!!!!! – You position yourself to operate in the overflow. Understanding the value of both Good Success and the "VDC Ten Step Business Protocol" is imperative. It allows you to equip your tactical business toolkit with a tome of knowledge.

I am excited about your future. The goal of this book is to transfer my many years of business acumen, insight, and wisdom to those who desire to operate in the overflow.

I know you are excited about your future, but before we move too swiftly; I let us align on how I perceive the essence or quintessence of *success*.

There is *"success"* and then there is *"good success."* I want to make sure you understand the difference between success and good success. In my business sphere, the difference between success and good success often lies in the depth and quality of the achievement.

Success generally refers to achieving a goal or reaching a desired outcome. It can come or go. It can be temporal or extended. It is often measured by external factors such as wealth, recognition, or status. It can be celebrated by influencers, or damaged by competitors and foes.

Good success, on the other hand, encompasses the positive fulfilment of success, but it also exemplifies a more holistic and fulfilling form of achievement. It not only includes reaching desired goals, but it reflects achieving those objectives in a way that brings personal satisfaction, ethical integrity, and positive impact for yourself as well as others. It is driven by achievement and purpose, but its' motivational foundation is veracity and probability. It has a proven track record, and it is crafted and designed to create a long-term legacy because it is fueled by unwavering faith. *Good Success* is not singularly focused, it is a multifaceted business strategy that yields triumph and attainment.

In essence, when I examine the path to *success*, it only becomes reality when there is a commitment to leadership.

While *success* might be about what you achieve in life, *good success* is about how you achieve it and the positive effects it has on your life and those who are influenced by you. It reflects the value that you create in the marketplace not only for your organization but your employees and partners.

I have chosen the path of *Good Success* for me. So, with that in mind...... Let's Start Stepping forward in order capture *"Good in Success"*.

Table of Content

Prolog

DR.VALERIE DANIELS-CARTER

Prolog

Leadership

The **VDC 10 Step Business Protocol** is designed to be a business guide for individuals who are preparing to start or grow their business. It outlines ten (10) vital questions that one must be able to intelligently and succinctly answer.

Additionally, you should be prepared to discuss and purposefully defend your conclusions in every area prior to making any final business decisions. If you cannot clearly articulate and defend your assumptions and facts, you may want to reconsider your path and determine if you are indeed ready to move forward.

> ➤ *Nugget - It is best to get things right upfront than to pay the cost of poor planning along the way.*

The title of this book, "Wherever I Go, Success Meets Me", it's not about self-promotion or pride, it really is about leadership and strategic planning.

To be a successful leader, one must understand the principles and true essence of leadership. Success will only go where it is taken. It has no legs or feet; it can only be directed by those who dare to defy the odds and who demand that greatness partners with them.

The foundational basis for the *VDC 10 Step Business Protocol* is ignited by those who embrace and personify the characteristics and traits of a genuine leader. For those who understand the value of doing what is necessary upfront to minimize unnecessary pitfalls.

When starting or expanding a business, leadership is key. As I often share with individuals, sometimes leadership might seem hard to completely define; but for most, it is easy to recognize. Successful leaders understand that the survival of an organization during periods of uncertainty depends not just on their technical ability to be task oriented, but it is also predicated on their tenacity and their ability to manage without disruption. It's predicted on how they are willing to navigate in their mission without compromise. It is dependent on their mandate to hold themselves responsible and accountable for all outcomes. Leaders do not look for excuses, they seek solutions.

Leadership isn't only about inspiring others; it is about knowing oneself. There are various personality types, and leadership skillsets, leadership is not a "one size fits all world".

Exceptional leaders understand that complacency is poison. It is a detriment and deterrent to greatness. Leaders must not be afraid to be transparent, it is critical that they make regular evaluations of his or her decisions. Leadership assessment tools provide practical steps that one can employ to measure his or her ability to manage and govern. It allows one to also determine what is needed for them to explore other relevant opportunities. It allows one to design their advanced business model based on their capability and competencies.

Being a leader is not always convenient or popular. Assessing your leadership success can sometimes be revealing and hurtful. You may think you have really accomplished something great, only to find out that you are not even close to achieving what is needed

Leaders must take time to measure and assess their successes as well as failures. The use of leadership assessment tools goes beyond the fact that they are just helpful, but they are critical. I compare it to going to the doctor for a checkup. You may not be sick, but you annually check in with your physician to ensure your health and wellness. It is acutely important for one to test his or her leadership skills against a defined baseline. This helps you see where you stand and allows you to challenge yourself to reach a higher or greater dimension of success. *The VDC Protocol for Business Success* is a strategic business leadership guide. If utilized as designed, it becomes a compendium for business success.

Henry Mintzberg, Professor of Management at McGill University, in an interview with the Harvard Business Journal is quoted as saying, "You don't become a manager in a classroom, and you certainly don't become a leader in a classroom." He states that, "Leadership is earned based on people who choose to follow you. It is not achieved because some school awards you a degree."

I believe that a Corporate Leader or Entrepreneur must consistently gauge their ability to produce, to vanguard and assess their organization. They possess both direct, indirect and cross-sectional metrics that allow them to monitor, evaluate and gauge their success on an ongoing basis.

23

Leadership cannot lack direction. Leadership accepts full responsibility for failures, but utilizes them as a means for training, developing and creating a better plan.

A leader is like a rudder on a boat steering the ship and keeping it on course. But here is the key .... The boat cannot float without a sound hull; it would coast aimlessly without sails and wouldn't be able to catch the wind if it had no crew. This is just another way of saying that leadership is more than just giving orders, it's about recognizing that every component plays a vital part. It is about motivating the entire team to achieve the task!!!!!

A leader is responsible for developing an integrated team, then unambiguously defining the shared responsibility of each person and then holding each stakeholder responsible for delivering exceptional results on time and within budget. They then celebrate the accomplishments, correct any noncompliance while ensuring that every contributor is properly acknowledged.

There are certain commonalities that successful leaders possess. I want to share with you 10 similar attributes of most successful leaders possess. They self -assess themselves by acknowledging these important attributes and consciously ask themselves these vital questions:

1. Am I grounded and centered?

2. Am I aware and mindful?

3. Can I create solutions?

4. How analytical am I?

5. Can I properly evaluate and measure risk?

6. Can I generate a sense of urgency and create a platform of excitement?

7. How insightful am I?

8. Do I possess the ability to build cohesiveness?

9.   Can I motivate people, and Do I make others better?

10. Do I have a plan that will exceed expectations?

Forward-thinking leaders ponder on a consistent these types of questions.   In essence, when I reference the statement, "Success Meets Me", it simply is an indicator that if implemented properly, leadership protocols will cultivate good success.

Let us now begin our journey by stepping through the *VDC Ten Step Protocol*.

DR.VALERIE DANIELS-CARTER

Protocol Step 1

Define why this Business or Company is Important?

Every person is unique with a different set of goals, responsibilities, knowledge, and tolerance of risk, time, and energy. Consequently, the path you travel to reach your goals is personal and suited to you alone; it begins with determining your desired destination. Only you can define that for you.

I'm not that great at golf, but I do have a high-level of respect for those who play it well. Golf is a sport like no other. There is no one else to lean on; it is just you, your clubs, and a little ball that determines its outcome. This game teaches you some major life lessons if played correctly. One of the key lessons is focus. Once you know what shot you want to hit, it is important to commit to that shot visually and mentally. The other important thing during the swing is to envision where you want to land and never take your eyes off the ball.

Taking your eyes off the ball or losing focus on your target can be a major hindrance to success on the golf course. When your eyes move off the ball, it affects your head, and body placement. This in turn causes you to hit a poor shot, and at times causes you to miss the ball completely. If you want to hit a good shot, take time to define the plan and the importance of the business.

> ➤ *Nugget* – This is an investment, so your vision needs to be clear; Visine has not jurisdiction here.

Capturing the essence of an idea should always begin with writing the vision and making it plain.   It is very easy to look around, and try to find something tangible to grab hold of and believe in. But understanding the "RIGHT" opportunity for you is extremely important. Just because something is available, does not mean it is for you.

Over time the vision may expand and grow, but the essence of the encapsulated picturesque idea needs to be written. Our first protocol is "Define why this business or company is important?"

Capture in writing and define why you have determined that there is a critical need for this business or why expansion is important. Growing for the sake of growth is not logical or prudent, there needs to be purpose behind your motive and intent.

Define means to state or describe exactly the nature, scope or meaning of what is intended. Collins dictionary records that when you define something, you show, describe, or state clearly what it is and what its limits are or what it is like.

You should create an executive summary as well as an expanded description of why business is important.

Take a moment and write the vision:

_____

_____

_____

_____

_____

_____

_____

_____

_____

_____

_____

_____

_____

_____

_____

_____

_____

_____

_____

_____

_____

Now, in less than 20 words, state the highlight of the vision:

_____

_____

Did you define what your business will be and what it will do for your customers? If not, try it again.

_____

_____

_____

_____

_____

_____

_____

_____

_____

_____

_____

_____

In a competitive market, being unique matters immensely. By defining the things that the business does above all others in the field allows customers and partners alike to realize the potential it offers to their relationship. That definition could shape the way everyone views the company. As a business leader, I have learned to connect purpose to every decision.

It is wise to start a business that provides a unique product or service that will be in high demand. It is also important to start a business that you believe in. When you build from a deep sense of purpose and belief, you will share it passionately with everyone around you. You will ignite a fire and encourage others to come and watch it burn.

DR.VALERIE DANIELS-CARTER

Protocol Step 2

What is the Problem and Burning Platform?

Emotions and pride in ownership can sometimes cause us to ignore important key indicators. So, when identifying the void and defining the urgency of the need, use wisdom. Wisdom is the quality of having experience, knowledge, and good judgment; it is the quality of being wise. Wisdom is the soundness of an action or decision regarding the application of experience, knowledge, and good judgment. Wisdom is the application of Truth.

> ➤ *Nugget:* It is one thing to know the truth; but Wisdom intentionally uses it to access purpose.

Wisdom involves an integration of knowledge, experience, and deep understanding, as well as a tolerance for the uncertainties of life. The more knowledgeable you are, the greater your capacity to succeed will be if you use wisdom. So yes, deploy wisdom but remember wisdom is most beneficial when you also have understanding. Wise leaders learn from experience and knowledge.

During my years of teaching at a bible college, I would often share with my students that, "You can't learn from a closed book – you have to read and rightly divide the Word". This is because, instinctively, you can know something, but research and information confirm that belief. Once you have knowledge, wisdom can be ignited. Successful entrepreneurs build businesses that solve problems or address unfilled opportunities.

So, as you are defining the platform to examine the dire need for a business, ensure that the reality of the issue is relevant, highly important or germane to your stated objectives. Make sure you have properly identified the issue.

Identifying the problem is not always as simple as it sounds. In some cases, people might mistakenly identify the wrong source of a problem or see the issue from narrow lens. You may want to ask probing questions or do additional research to ensure that there indeed is a need.

For example, you may have a desire to establish a fitness facility. But if there are already three other fitness facilities within a narrowly defined radius, there might not be a need for an additional facility.

37

This is not a burning platform and honestly, I would encourage you to make sure that you understand the distinguishing difference before you invest capital in this new venture. This example would be an illustration of a desire, not a problem or need. As business leaders, we must understand what really is a "burning platform".

The concept of a "burning platform" comes from the analogy of standing on an oil platform at sea that's on fire - the urgency to save yourself is so great that you act and jump off. In business, burning platform is a term used to describe the process of helping people see the dire consequences of not making corrective adjustments or taking time to succinctly identify the issue. In other words, it is crucial that one creates or addresses the matter, while understating "what is the purpose?" The questions must be asked, why are you creating this business or modifying your plans, and why now? Why is there an urgency?

To understand if there is a burning platform, you must understand the difference between facts and beliefs. Opinions can be very costly if they are conveyed by an inexperienced source.

The key is to properly prove your belief and define the urgency and significance of need. This can be done by research, surveying and seeking varying views from qualified sources. This step usually involves generating as many ideas as possible without initially making judgment. Once several possibilities have been created, you then can evaluate and determine what is meaningful.

Before coming up with a solution, you need to first organize the available information. What do you know about the problem? What do you *not* know? The more information that is available the better prepared you will be to formulate an accurate solution.

When approaching a problem, it is important to make sure that you have all the data you need. Take the time to do it right. Deciding on how to move forward without having adequate information can restrict your success and often produce disappointing outcomes. I cannot emphasize enough the importance of understanding the difference between an actual need verses a strong desire.

> *Nugget:* Where there is no need, there is no opportunity.

One of the reasons that some ideas never reach their potential is because the idea was never fully and properly vetted or analyzed. This is where concepts such as a "decision tree" come in handy by allowing the simulations of various paths and steps. A decision tree starts with the root of the matter and then defines all the branches of possibility.

If done properly, most ideas can be accurately assessed and evaluated. Problem identification requires time, commitment, resourcefulness, flexibility, resilience, and continuous review of the challenge. If there is a genuine problem, you may wish it to go away, but it must be managed, because problems do not disappear overnight without being properly resolved. Many times, they linger and remind you of the void each time you think about it. They continue to burn through even in the mist of adversity. It is not difficult to recognize or identify glaring deficiencies, because posers are always looking for someone smart enough to solve them. The key is properly identifying and defining it for what it truly is.

Here is a simple tool. The 5W (what) 2H (How) method. This method forces us to ask seven basic questions: Who, What, When, Where Why, How, and How much or How many.

The framework for the 5W2H is:

1. Who? Who are the people impacted by the Problem? Who caused it? Who may know more about it?

2. What? What is your current situation, your desired situation, and the gap between them?

3. When? When did the problem occur? Is it on-going? Will it happen again in the future?

4. Where? Where is the location of your problem?

5. Why? Why did the problem occur or why does it continue to occur? Why is the problem important to address?

6. How? How could you solve the problem? What process should you use?

7. How much or how many? How big is the problem? How much harm is it causing? How long will it take to solve?

Looking at the void and gap of any situation allows you to assess future capacity and worth. The goal is to ensure that your company will solve a need. A burning platform encourages modification or development. It is a solution-oriented model that encourages a businessperson to understand and anticipate what the future will be and what the opportunity will yield if all is achieved.

Once you have determined that you should move forward. Don't become distracted. With so many voices in our lives sometimes we become distracted by simple nonessential things. With our fast-paced life, stopping, pausing, being patient, and calm seems to be a thing of the past. But when you are confident that you are ready to move forward and you are assured that you have received good advice, collected accurate information and have designed a strong product offering. It's time to continue to put the remaining pieces in place. Don't allow yourself to become weary in well doing. It takes time to build a sustainable business. There is a season called reaping, and you will reap if you faint not.

DR.VALERIE DANIELS-CARTER

Protocol Step 3

Who is the customer?

Who is the customer? Do you really understand, or can you properly define who your customer is? Your customer can vary depending on the circumstance and product. We recently started a wonderful company here in Wisconsin. It is an exciting opportunity. After hiring the lead manager, I asked him, *"who do you really think is your customer"?* He began to dialog with me whom he thought to be his customer. I listened and then explained to him that what he was describing was just a portion or one segment of his true customer base.

Segmentation of the need helps you to define your customer for a defined service or product. Segmentation of the service will also help you to analyze the needs of your customer. You may have multiple customers. Your customer may be a corporate client, if so, you would structure or design products to address their needs. Your customer may be a consumer or an individual and you may have other services, products or promotions designed for that individual. Believe it or not, your customer may be someone that is closely related in the same business as yours. This is called "B to B" a (Business to Business) relationship. The key is to understand the protocol behind each customer and properly identify the needs for that individual or that organization.

In essence, the customer is who you ae trying to service in order to redeem something from them. It can be redeemed not just in a financial way, but it also can be redeemed in other ways of bartering. Here is the essence of this protocol:

1. Understand the individual or organization.

2. Define a structure that addresses their needs.

3. Understand the protocol for properly servicing them.

Many of you know that I am in the restaurant business. Some may think my customer is just the person that comes to our restaurant and orders a soft pretzel with pepperoni. Yes, that is just one of my customers. For that customer, we have designed a display case to entice them to purchase the greatest pretzels in the world.

On the other hand, we have a restaurant at the airport. In this case, my customers are not only the passengers, but other individuals that work within the airport environment. Many times, we create different offerings for airport employees to keep them coming day after day. We must be able to offer variety, special discounts, and other incentives to service this customer.

Most often, the customer is defined by the need, but we may service them based on categorization or segmentation.

To establish, protect and defend your position in the market, you must have the ability to know who you are working for, while creating, building and maintaining strong customer relationships with those individuals or organizations. This helps to preserve their interest and ensure your product or service is viewed as fulfilling their need.

As an emerging business owner, I know you are enthusiastic about your business and confident about what it has to offer. But it is important to recognize that everyone is not your customer. Believing that everyone is your customer is counterproductive. You cannot afford to spend time, energy and money trying to reach people who your product or service is not intended for, or those who aren't interested in what you have to offer. So many business owners lose thousands of dollars trying to attract the wrong client base. To sustain your business, you must understand who your customer is truly.

> ➢ *Nugget* – Where there is no interest, there is no desire.

To build a thriving business, you must put time, attention, and effort into improving customer experience. Customers are the heart of a business; when satisfied with your products and service, they return and generally bring other new customers to experience your product or service.

Identifying and understanding your customers' preferences allows you to deliver superior service and exceed the expectations of your customers. It builds a strong business reputation, drives sales, improves brand awareness, increases conversion rate, and helps business growth.

There are several ways of getting to know your customers, but ways are as follows:

1. Put yourself in their place.

2. Use Customer Relationship Management (CRM) tools.

3. Ask for feedback and what they think about you.

Things you can do to determine your customer base can be as simple as having conversation and dialogue with your current customer base. If you do not have any customers, create a survey to determine the types of individuals that would be drawn to your business or service.

You can gather information on your current customers through Google Analytics and social media insights. Also, determine which social media platforms your customers use most often. Don't be afraid to enlist the help of social media listening and sentiment analysis tools to see what customers on these platforms need.

Identify and look for platforms where your product or services are most requested. Also, create a buzz for your product based on defined market segmentation.

I have never seen a business succeed without having strong external connectivity and advantageous external relations. Strong customer relationships are the building blocks which assist you in defining and growing your customer base. Set growth targets for yourself.

Organizations today live in highly dynamic environments. Essentially the existence and growth of the businesses are market alignment which can be highly segmented geographical markets. So, it is important to know where your customer resides. It might be difficult to sell a winter coat in Florida during October, but you can aggressively target Minnesota in that month and build a relatively strong customer base. Customer growth and development goes hand in hand with your ability to manage positive relationships, whether your relationship is with a vendor, supplier, servicer, investor, donor or client. Your customer is more than just your end user.

Technology, the internet as well as globalization are redefining how we engage with new customers. To be competitive in the current marketplace, you need retail, online and mobile customers. Because of the changing of the marketplace, it is essential that you target those individuals who are users of your product or services.

DR. VALERIE DANIELS-CARTER

Protocol Step 4

What is the Solution and What value does the Solution Create?

In preparing yourself to start or grow your business, one must clearly understand and evaluate the importance and cost associated with beginning this venture or expanding your business platform. What is the significance of extending this service or product and will it be meaningful. When you are seriously engaged in formulating an organization, it is more than just doing something as a hobby.

You must examine the business proposition and establish what your business model should be. It is important to take time to properly identify the right business model.

A business model is a written strategy for making a profit. It identifies the products or services the business plans to sell. It identifies target markets, and any anticipated expenses. Business models are important for both new and established businesses. They help companies attract investment, recruit talent, and motivate management and staff.

Your business model should define the value that the solution will yield. When you determine what the solution is based on the need, the monetization of the solution will yield a determined value. It is important to build your model with all the necessary components, such as the products or services the business plans to sell. It ensures the right target markets and creates financial projections which include both revenues and expenses. Two very important levers of a business model are pricing and costs. Analysts and investors often look at a company's gross profit to evaluate the success of a business model.

> ➤ *Nugget* – If you don't plan on generating a profit, then it is either a hobby or a charitable contribution.

A business model should be periodically revised to make sure it still reflects the business environment and customer demands.

Once you define your business model you should let it be your guiding tool. You may adjust your strategy from time to time but try your best to remain committed to your core intent.

Be careful not to get stretched in the wrong direction and do things haphazardly.

On occasion, business owners will have trouble and may irrationally act based on the circumstances. I would advise you to stay on the course and address matters based on your business model and your good judgment. Pause and process, don't become over reactionary over a situation, it may only require a minor adjustment.

As a business leader, you must stay focused. Success does not happen overnight. Remember as you are outlining your business plan, incorporate ranges that address both the highs and lows of your business.

When you don't stay focused and committed to your plan, you will be all over the place, and you will limit your ability to produce. Your level of frustration and stress will be heightened. I challenge you to build confidence in what you have designed, knowing that you have modeled it based on the customer's need. Always work to ensure that you are creating value. You are a businessperson. You are in business. So, you must understand and manage the expected, unexpected and what is realized.

Value is not always the lowest price or the highest level of profit. It can also be defined by the upliftment and culture created for someone. This is a true story. Annually my organization used to have year-end events to celebrate our high achievers. I would often invite the low achievers, so that they could experience the benefit of those who met or exceeded corporates benchmarks.

> ➤ *Nugget* – Sometimes a non-performer, must be shown what performance looks and feels like.

During these leadership dinners, we dress in our finest attire, and we take time to formally acknowledge and celebrate winners. One year one of our exceptional operators was invited to the dinner to be acknowledged. She was dressed from her head to her feet, and she thought she was 'miss it and a bunch of chips". She thought she had it going on, and of course me as being Mrs. Carter, and wanting everybody to feel good about themselves, I embraced her and gave her a hug. But my sister, who was serving as the hostess that evening, did not have the same demeanor. When she noticed how the young lady was dressed, she could not help but laugh. My sister Hattie loved making jabs. She loved telling jokes and having fun. But because I have a sensitivity to people, even when they are not looking like what they think they look like; I will still find a way to say something positive. It might be something like, "girl you better go ahead."

As the evening went on, my sister, who had literally fallen out laughing earlier about this outfit, began acknowledging the winners. When this manager's name was called, Hattie looked at me. For the sake of safety, let's call her, "I am dressed to kill." My sister, called Ms. I am dressed to kill's name.

When Ms. I am dressed to kill walked up to receive her award and acknowledgements. Hattie, who could not help herself asked, "Where did you get this $1,000,000 dress from. With great pride and joy, Ms. I am dressed to kill said the name of the store she had bought the dress from. Instead of my sister saying to her you really look nice and letting her go back to her seat. My sister said, "girl, I need you to model this dress for everybody". Even though initially, people were laughing and almost bursting into tears, Ms. I am dressed to kill, exhumed an air of confidence as she began to strut up and down the aisle. People started applauding and cheering her because of her radiant smile, exuberant and catching personality, and her noted accomplishments. They no longer looked at what she had on, but they recognized her strength and her ability. She knew who she was and what she had accomplished. She created her own value platform, one that to this day, we all still acknowledge.

> ➤ *Nugget* – When you feel good about yourself (your company, your product), it resonates with others, and they will have to acknowledge your positivity and accomplishments.

By the time she finished her champion's walk, we were all standing and applauding her. Her perception of herself did not change because of the environment. She knew her merit and self-worth and with sincerity she conveyed why she indeed was a winner.

She did not allow what others may have thought to change her perception of herself to win. When I closed the event, I shared with our entire team the idea of understanding your value and how it will drive unexpected results.

A business model is how you do what you do to generate posture and profit. It is the value proposition that you as the entrepreneur have defined. People can duplicate your product or service, but they cannot duplicate your model, because it is unique to you and your business. It may be similar in style, but your vision and uniqueness are your distinguishing factors. If position correctly, your solution will ultimately yield strong results and profits.

DR.VALERIE DANIELS-CARTER

Protocol Step 5

What is the Business Model

A business model is a high-level plan for successfully operating a business in a specific marketplace. A primary component of the business model is the value proposition. A business model is a company's core strategy for profitably doing business. It is inclusive of their offerings, products or services which the business plans to offer or sell. It is one of the components of their overall business plan. It defines ones: 1) target market, 2) structure and 3) anticipated financial obligations. Business models are important for both new and established businesses. They help new and developing companies attract investment, recruit talent, and motivate management and staff. Established businesses must regularly update their business model to remain current and relative. If they fail to anticipate trends and market challenges, it could have an adverse effect on the business.

The Business Model is the pictorial view of the business; the Business Plan is the executable outline of the business. The model is the mold, the Plan outlines the actionable events.

There are as many types of business models as there are types of businesses. For instance, direct sales, franchising, advertising-based, and brick-and-mortar stores are all examples of traditional business models. There are federations, nonprofit entities, regional and nationally develop concepts. There are also hybrid models as well…. such as businesses that combine internet retail with brick-and-mortar stores or with sporting organizations like the NBA. There are business models that solely focus only on the internet.

The one thing they all have in common is that to thrive, there must be a business plan in place with set or expected outcomes which define the associated cost, the expected revenue which enables the business to be managed profitably. A common mistake many companies make when they create their business models is that they underestimate the costs of operating or maintaining the business until it becomes profitable or sustainable.

I often tell business leaders, "Never sign a Blank check". Make sure you have complete knowledge of all costs associated with a venture.

When the pandemic hit America, businesses were forced to minimize their in-person staffing. For companies in America, it was a difficult period. Very few organizations had prepared a strategy for transitioning into a hybrid workplace. There were no budgets allocated to expanded IT and virtual work environments. This was a very difficult changeover for most companies not just in America, but Worldwide. Coming up with strategies to ensure a continuum of offering of services for most organizations requires employees and leaders to think and manage in a different manner. In many cases, most small businesses were not technologically equipped to handle online work platforms. Additionally, there was a learning curve for many of their customers. Also, ministries were significantly affected. They had to take on a different business model. Our local ministry had parishioners who desired to come to our physical location. Because of this, leaders had to be creative, and we were forced to create an alternative operating strategy. In discussion with our leaders, we decided to create a hybrid experience for this group of believers. An experience was created called "Park Up Worship".

"Park Up Worship". In doing so, it required our finance team to determine the total cost of offering an external public parking ministry service. This involved understanding the type of system that would be needed, identifying technicians who could operate and manage a broad base system for external use, examining methods to ensure sound quality, and how cars would be placed. We had to purchase equipment to allow a strong FM broadband for the interior of cars and an exterior projection system that could cast clear video. There were other considerations, such as marketing and communicating to our members this new way to experience our services. The deeper we dived, the greater the cost became. It was more than just telling perishers to drive up and park. After doing a giving vs cost analysis, it was determined that offering this service would be both spiritually and financially beneficial.

> *Nugget* – Know the amount before you write the check.

In creating the business model, it is important to identify the legal structure and the benefits thereof. Business structure refers to the legal structure of an organization that is recognized in each jurisdiction.

An organization's legal structure is a key determinant of the activities that it can undertake, such as raising capital, responsibility for obligations of the business, as well as the amount of taxes that the organization owes to tax agencies.

Before making a choice on the type of legal structure, business owners should first consider their needs and goals and understand the features of each business structure.

There are seven main forms of business structures in the United States [2]. They are:

Sole Proprietorship

Limited Liability Company (LLC)

General Partnership (GP)

Limited Partnership (LP)

Corporation (C Corp, B Corp, and S Corps)

Nonprofit Organization

Cooperative (co-op)

Having sound legal advice in advance will allow you to manage, understand and adhere to necessary regulatory requirements. Again, doing something after the fact only opens you up to rework and possible unnecessary claims.

DR.VALERIE DANIELS-CARTER

Protocol Step 6

What is the financial model?

One of the methods by which analysts and investors evaluate the success of a business model is by looking at the company's gross profit. Gross profit is a company's total revenue minus the cost of goods sold (COGS). Comparing a company's gross profit to that of its main competitor or its industry sheds light on the efficiency and effectiveness of its business model. Gross profit alone can be misleading, that is why analysts and investors also want to see cash flow or net income. Your cash flow is the gross profit minus operating expenses and is an indication of just how much real profit the business is generating.

Having good financial health eases pressure on the operator, allows for growth and expansion and allows you to properly manage.

Typical signs of strong financial health within a business include:

➢ A steady flow of income

➢ Rare changes in expenses

➢ Strong returns on investments

➢ A cash balance that is growing

To improve your financial health, you need to:

➢ Assess your current net worth

➢ Create a budget you can stick to

➢ Build an emergency fund

➢ Pay down your debts

It is key to staying keenly focused and ensuring you have a business and financial model that breeds success.

There is an increasing need for business leaders to be able to forecast and plan with agility in order to be prepared for increasing economic volatility. Therefore, your financial model should define best case scenarios, expected results and worse case scenarios. You always want to stay ahead of your projections.

An important and durable lesson of recent worldwide massive disruptions has led us to understand that organizations need to forecast and plan with external intelligence to quickly adapt to evolving economic, market, legal, regulatory, and behavioral conditions. If you are in the logistics business, a shut-down in the transportation industry could have a massive impact on your ability to meet your targets.

> ➤ *Nugget*: **Plan for health, not just wealth.**

Wealth can be here today and gone tomorrow.

As you build on this protocol, having a realistic proforma that identifies various levels or stages of operations is important. You may be in a business that is seasonal, understanding the months that you generate your highest level of profits as well as the lean months are critical. Do not build "blue sky" into your proforma or projection. You want it to be as realistic as possible, identifying all the costs associated with operating your business. Failure to understand the overall cost to operate your business will cause adverse results.

It may not seem like much initially, but every quarter of a point matters in business, every wasted dollar can prevent you from achieving your overall goal. The hidden costs of waste, repetitive training and mismanagement in many cases is the difference between having a mediocre business versus a very successful company.

If you are not good at forecasting and financial planning, I would advise you to get a good CPA to assist you in this area. I can't emphasize enough the importance of knowing your financial performance on an ongoing basis. You should not wait until the end of the month or the end of the quarter to determine how you are managing. It is healthy to have a day-to-day report on your key financial indicators. I have come to learn that nothing spends faster than money. Lastly make sure you always maintain a savings reserve for your company. Set aside a portion of your profits for capital expenditures, new business concepts, and corporate reserves.

> *Nugget* - It is important that you prepare before the storm, because when you're in the midst of the wind everything seems out of control

Protocol Step 7

What is the Channel to Market?

.

To access and define an exceptional channel to market, a company must have a strong and astute leader and exceptional marketing strategy. They must understand the various ways to access the end user. They may choose a direct sales and marketing approach, or channel marketing.

A direct sales and marketing approach generally means you and your team will take responsibility for the branding and selling of your product or service. You can use various sales channels and portals to advance your business, like direct mail, social media, automated email marketing, special events, telecommunication or any type of method needed to access exposure and touch points for the benefit of sales and business growth.

Channel Marketing is a practice that involves having other parties (either businesses or individuals) sell your product or service.

So, you have now established a wonderful organization, how do you ensure marketing success and access market channels.

Let's start first with marketing a new or emerging business. There is a plethora of reasons why one should ensure one is properly marketing one's business.

Marketing visibility informs your customers about your product offering or services. It builds and maintains brand reputation. It curates and delivers a consistent marketing message that shapes a strong, recognizable brand identity for your organization. Strong marketing can sustain your business relevancy and create long-term and loyal customers.

Direct or internal marketing of a business maintains the relevance of the organization. The goal of marketing is to convince a person that your product is worth investing in, to establish brand loyalty and increase overall sales. Marketing is foundational and is paramount for any business. It drives visibility and places a business in the eye of the customer. Innovation thrives when combined with insightful marketing. Together, they ensure that products reach the desired audience, resonate with them, and remain financially viable for the company. For a business to thrive, an effective marketing strategy is non-negotiable. It is about more than just promoting products; but it is about crafting a narrative, maintaining a dialogue with your audience and building and maintaining strong relationships.

> ➤ *Nugget:* You can have a great product; but if no one is aware of your product or service, it's just an expensive placeholder.

Next let's discuss Channel Marketing. Channel marketing involves using different distribution channels to sell and market your products or services. Channel marketing partners help you sell the advantages of your product to customers. The channel partners you work with in channel marketing are generally groups like consultants, agents, distributors, resellers, affiliates, connected members association, and other types of third-party companies. Building good relationships with these partners is critical to the overall success of your company if you choose this route as your marketing platform. The key to channel marketing is a mutually beneficial relationship between you and your channel marketing partners.

Channel marketing differs from just promoting your product through advertising and marketing channels. Generally, channel partners are also businesses or companies. When you create a platform of multiple channel partners, you really have multiple separate companies promoting or selling the same product.

The key benefit of channel marketing is that your products can reach audiences you would otherwise not have access to.

The channel partners benefit is that they earn a percentage of the product sales or a discount on bulk purchases that they resell.

This can be a win-win situation in that channel marketing is a way for you and your partners to help each other reach the same goal—to sell and help people. Most small businesses do not have the capacity to have a fully developed marketing department, or the resources to dedicate funding for a sales team. They may not have the capacity to do international marketing or have a global or even multi-state reach. If you partner with the right partners and there is a demand for your product, this is a much more cost-effective way to do broaden your marketing reach.

Amazon is a perfect example of channel marketing. The product goes from manufacturer to amazon, and from Amazon to consumer. The manufacturer has no direct contact with the customer. They just produce products for Amazon to sell and promote.

When choosing your channel marketing partners, whether resellers, affiliates, consultants, distributors to promote your product of service, you should be able to answer two questions:

1. What's in it for them?
2. What's in it for you?

Once you determine that you have the right partner and it is a win / win situation, then you can move forward.

Here are a few points to review when looking for a potential channel marketing partner:

1. Ability to strategize: Can they see both the big picture and smaller details of your channel marketing relationship? Are they willing to strategically position you to win?
2. Similar goals: A partner's goals should work with your own, and you should understand the goals before you commit to a partnership.

3.   Able to adapt to change: Are you going to be able to agree on necessary changes when a plan needs to change? Are you open to changing the price of your product to meet the customer's needs?

4.   Proof of growth: What kind of growth has this potential partner accomplished in their business? Can they speak about specific sales and marketing goals they could help you meet? Are they willing to provide added value

5.   to your business?

6.   Proof of motivation: You want a partner who will actively contribute to your channel marketing plan, not someone who waits to be told what to do. You need them to push for success with you.

Being actively involved and keeping the process simple drives new business to your partners and keeps them loyal to you. Overall, you must determine the best marketing strategy for your business. The key is identifying what works best for your company, and making sure it is properly communicated to everyone within your organization.

DR.VALERIE DANIELS-CARTER

Protocol Step 8

Who are your Competitors?

This question is posed daily, and the answer can change faster than we can even imagine. With over 33.3 million small businesses in America, you are likely to have several competitors. But determining who truly will have an impact on what you do is key.

When I started looking at the US Bureau of Labor statistics, there were so many industry categories until I closed the search engine. But what it did for me strengthened my belief that a person really needs to make sure they understand their business, competitor, and opportunity. Your next-door neighbor might be your new competitor tomorrow.

A competitor is generally defined as someone or something that strives to achieve the same shared outcome. It is between two or more individuals or companies. As an astute businessperson, you must take the time to identify and pinpoint your competitors. You can determine who your competitors are by researching local directories, contacting your local chamber of commerce, contacting the National chamber of commerce, googling online research, looking at press reports and articles that reference your service or product, attending various trade fairs and exhibitions. You can also ask your customers and the media and marketing companies within your area about any potential competitors.

Your competitors can be online organizations who distinguish themselves as the "expert" within a certain industry or field.

Anyone you believe will attract customers from your business as well as companies or organizations that you will have to share the market with, is your competitor. They come in all sizes, large and small. Their goal is to gain market share and dominate. Therefore, you must be intentional in identifying who they are and creating a strategy to protect and grow your share.

Competitors will create marketing programs to divert the customer to them. In the burger business, competitors will deeply discount a product to drive traffic and entice a customer. You must always ensure you have a compelling reason why your customer either stays or quickly returns.

There are generally three types of competitors that you want to ensure that you focus on as you analyze your competition. The goal is to understand how to best vanguard against your competition and position yourself for success.

The first is Direct Competition (DC). Direct competition is generally defined as a company that offers a similar solution to a similar audience and in a similar way within a similar geography. An example of this might be Home Depot, Lowes, Fleet Farm and Menards. If I need to purchase a kitchen sink, I would compare companies and their price, quality and availability.

The next is Indirect Competition (IC). The companies are in your category, but they solve the customer problem differently. An example of this might be Direct TV and Apple TV. I can pay for Direct TV, or I can download apps to get programming. In some cases, the direct competitor may offer multiple platforms. They do this to maintain their customers. An example of this might be Spectrum. They offer phone, WIFI and streaming services.

The last form of competition we will highlight is Replacement Competition (RD). These competitors are in a different category altogether but solve the same problem. A good example of this would be a hungry person who is looking for entertainment. They purchase a Bucks or Packers game ticket, but instead of going to a restaurant before the game, they go to the arena early and grab something to eat from the concessions.

Once you define your competitor, then you should make sure you complete a competitor analysis about them and your business. Do not be afraid to list your weaknesses and strengths. It will allow you to become better. Knowing your competitor really isn't about them, it's about you, and your ability to have rival knowledge which can drive strong results for your company.

> ➢ *Nugget* - Leaders are extremely passionate about what they do, how they do it, and when they do it.

Protocol Step 9

What are the risks and the Risk Mitigation Approach?

In essence, Risk Mitigation is a strategy to prepare for and reduce the effects of threats faced by a business. Many times, we fail to measure or properly understand the effects some inherent dangers can have on our business and on our employees. Understanding the occurrences or things that could jeopardize or endanger your business, or ministry is fundamentally important to your overall success. Wise businesspeople and corporate leaders are astute enough to put in place safeguards and measurements that lessen or prevent major occurrences. And if disruption occurs, because of the mitigation strategy that has been properly vetted, the effect is significantly reduced.

> ➢ *Nugget:* - Don't become too comfortable because things are going extremely well, because a sleeping giant will ultimately be defeated.

To the degree you can reduce or eliminate problems, you want to do that.

There are certain threats that pose significant risk to a business. They include but are not limited to ...... cyberattacks, weather events, social or environmental events and other causes of physical or virtual damage. Also, there could be the risk of staffing of people, product supply or external or internal traps or various media influences. The key is to always try to be prepared for any major change or occurrence. Never get too comfortable just because things are going well. Eventually something is going to happen to burst the bubble.

There is a difference in Risk Avoidance and Risk Mitigation. Risk Avoidance is to shift into a different place to avoid a situation or threat, Risk Mitigation deals with the aftermath of a disaster and the steps that can be taken prior to the event occurring to reduce adverse and, potentially, long-term effects.

I was involved in an organization that had a very strong and proficient senior management team that delivered year-over-year exceptional results. The sleeping giant in the room was that the entire leadership team was tenured; all around the same age and their retirement requests were all within a year of each other.

Because of the board's failure to properly plan for succession in a timely manner, we had to put in place an immediate Risk Mitigation plan for succession once we learned of the closeness of the transition dates. We were too late for Risk Avoidance in the case of this management team. Therefore, we had to shift into a Risk Mitigation mode. This happens all too often in business environments.

As business and ministry leaders, you must create a strong culture around risk management. This means communicating the values, attitudes and beliefs surrounding risk and compliance from the top down. It's important for every employee or ministry worker to have risk awareness. The probability of a strong culture is greatly improved when management or ministry leaders set the tone. Risk mitigation is the process of planning for disasters and having a way to lessen negative impacts, it is important to weigh the impact of each risk and prioritize planning around that impact. Risk mitigation focuses on the predictability of some disasters and is used for those situations where a threat cannot be avoided entirely.

Here are five steps for creating your Risk Mitigation Plan:

> Identify the Risk

> Perform a Risk Assessment

➤ Prioritize the highest areas of risk for the Risk Assessment

➤ Define the Plan and Implement

➤ Track and Monitor the Progress of the Plan

There are many other key strategies in this area that I would encourage you to explore.

DR.VALERIE DANIELS-CARTER

Protocol Step 10

What is the Exit Strategy?

An e**xodus or exit strategy** is a contingency plan that is executed by an investor, trader, venture capitalist, and business owner or ministry leader when it is time to retire, sell or liquidate a position or business. A **business exit strategy** is an entrepreneur's strategic plan to sell their ownership in a company to investors or another company. It gives a business owner a way to reduce or liquidate their stake in a business and, if the business is successful, it allows them to capture the value upon their transfer. It is a strategic way to consciously plan for the next opportunity. It allows you to plan for capturing value. An Exit Strategy is defined and carefully planned. There are many things to consider as you ponder through your exit strategy, such as:

➢ How much control do you want to maintain?

➢ Do you want continued involvement?

➢ What is the best or proper way to cash out?

➢ What is the best way to transfer ownership?

➢ Who are the key players or organizations that are needed to execute the strategy?

These are the key thoughts; I am certain there are many more.

Common types of Exit Strategies include Initial Public Offerings (IPO), Strategic Acquisitions, and Management Buy-Outs (MBO). A key aspect of an Exit Strategy is Business Valuation or the valuation of the business. There are specialists that can help business owners (and buyers) examine a company's financials to determine fair value. There are also transition managers whose role is to assist sellers with their business exit strategies.

For leaders determining the best transitional time is key and critical. Identifying on-going roles and responsibilities are important. So often, we fail to mentor the next leader at the appropriate time. When you are burned out- that is too late.

It would not be me if I did not share a principle from one of the greatest books in the world, the bible.

We learn **in I Kings 19:21 (KJV) [3]** the story of Elijah and Elisha. It reads as follows: *"And he returned back from him, and took a yoke of oxen, and slew them, and boiled their flesh with the* *instruments of the oxen, and gave unto the people, and they did eat. Then he arose, and went after Elijah, and ministered unto him. "*

To me, this is one of the greatest mentorship stories of all times. It reflects both the role of the protégé and the mentor. In his first encounter with Elijah, Elisha is willing to let go of his occupation, his family, and the life he had built thus far to follow a man who he desired to mentor him. He killed his oxen and destroyed the yoke, giving the proceeds to his neighborhood. This would be the equivalent of selling a business and throwing a party with the proceeds.

Bible scholars believe that Elisha served Elijah for six years before Elijah was ushered into Heaven. So much can be learned by observing the life of another. We can learn from their habits and disciplines, how they relate to others, and even from their faults. Elisha was destined for a double portion but had to first offer himself as a servant leader. If he had not offered himself as a servant to Elijah, he would have remained a farmer and never performed the amazing miracles that blessed the lives of so many others.

Don't limit your capacity to expand and grow, based solely on where you are today. Transitioning or exiting is not a bad thing, especially when you are comfortable that you have achieved your objectives.

➤ *Nugget* – to exit means you have walked through a pathway, just make sure it was worth it.

DR.VALERIE DANIELS-CARTER

Conclusion

My goal in writing this book was to provide a proven foundational protocol for starting or expanding your business. Over the years, I have been asked by entrepreneurs, "Where do I start". It is my hope that this book will be a guide for those who are visionary leaders.

Understanding the business platform before you set launch is critical. It shapes better decisions, fosters empathy, and prevents unnecessary mistakes. Knowledge is the foundation upon which thoughtful actions are built, and it's through understanding that we can navigate complexities with confidence and purpose.

Having a great idea is the beginning of the journey. If you are going to be a contender in this very competitive world of business, you must be committed to doing everything that is necessary to have a first-class organization. Every leader is not a business owner; some people are better equipped to manage and care for their vision, and some are designed to be the second chair. You must know your skill and your capacity. There is great value in both. Be secure enough to play your role. You can never live comfortably in a house that was not designed as your home. Understand that in life, there are different assignments and different giftings; each is important. You are responsible for your territory. Don't get distracted by getting in a race that was not designed for you to run. Be strong and have good courage.

To achieve and build a strong business, you don't have to be the smartest, most talented, or someone who is connected to the "who's who" in life. You just need to be a visionary front runner that is not afraid to champion unchartered territory or have a compelling or unique product or proposition. Be one who is disciplined and consistent and maintain intentionality as you pursue for success.

Let me highlight Ten Paradoxical Commandments of Leadership [4] that I strive to live by.

- ❖ If you do good, people will accuse you of selfish ulterior motives— Do Good Anyway.

- ❖ If you're successful, you'll win false friends and true enemies— But Succeed Anyway.

- ❖ The good you do today will perhaps be forgotten tomorrow— But you Must Do Good Anyway.

- ❖ Honesty and frankness make you vulnerable— But Be Honest and Frank Anyway.

- ❖ The biggest man with the biggest ideas can be shot down by the smallest man with the smallest mind— But Think Big Anyway.

- ❖ People favor underdogs but follow only hot dogs— But you continue to fight for Underdogs Anyway.

❖ What you spend years building may be destroyed overnight— But Keep Building Anyway.

❖ People really need help but may refuse your assistance— But Help Them Anyway.

❖ If you get kicked to the curb while trying to give your best— Just Keep Giving your Best Anyway.

❖ Always remember, if better is possible - then Good is Not Enough.

Why - - - - - -

Because Leadership Takes Courage, Independence and Instinct. Excellence and Greatness are by design and leaders model their results based on those two plateaus, coupled with God's grace.

References

[1] - Copyright © 2024 ◆ Commerce Institute

[2] - www.financialtreecompany.com

Copyright © Taxguru.inc

[3] - 2024 King James Bible Online™

[4] - THE PARADOXICAL COMMANDMENTS OF LEADERSHIP By Kent Keith. New Zealand Planning Institute.

Edited by: Ensure Publishing

Final Book Edits by:

Dr. Aluap D. Sille

Jerome Pitchford

Made in the USA
Monee, IL
14 May 2026

50160390R00070